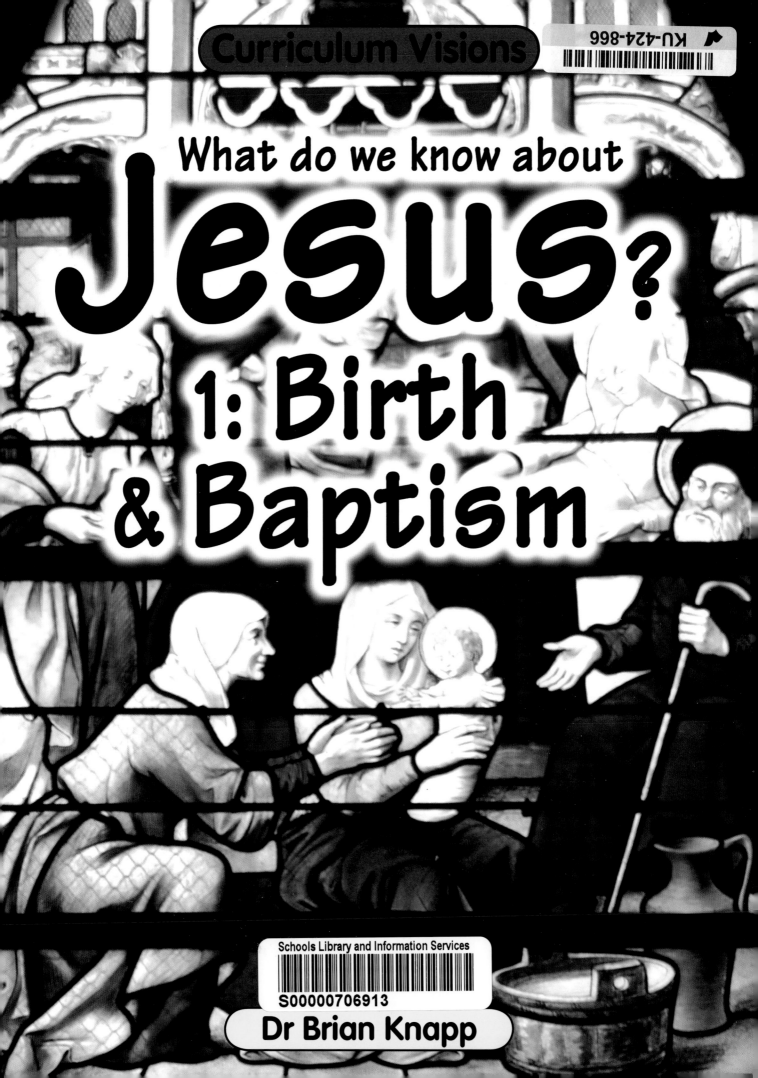

Curriculum Visions

What do we know about
Jesus?
1: Birth & Baptism

Dr Brian Knapp

The young Jesus in the Temple.

Notes

There are many translations and adaptations of the Bible. In this book we have sometimes used the King James version, but we have used many other versions and sometimes adapted them, too, depending on which seemed most appropriate for our reading level purpose and for the reading audience.

We have used capital letters to start words that refer to holy people, particularly Jesus or God (Him, He, etc). We have also used capitals when a particular event is implied, such as the Crucifixion of Jesus, but small letters when the general term is implied (e.g. crucifixion). This rule has also been applied to other holy people, such as Disciples (the 12) and disciples (general followers).

The opportunity has been taken to include works of art so that you can see the depiction of events in the eyes of some of the world's most famous historical and modern artists.

Curriculum Visions

There's much more online including videos

You will find multimedia resources covering a wide range of topics at:

www.CurriculumVisions.com

CurriculumVisions is a subscription web site.

A CVP Book © Earthscape 2009

Author
Brian Knapp, BSc, PhD

Researcher
Lisa Magloff, MA

Religious Advisor
The Revd Colin Bass, BSc, MA

Senior Designer
Adele Humphries, BA, PGCE

Editor
Gillian Gatehouse

Designed and produced by
EARTHSCAPE

Printed in China by
WKT Company Ltd

**What do we know about Jesus?
1: Birth & Baptism – Curriculum Visions
A CIP record for this book is
available from the British Library**

Paperback ISBN 978 1 86214 563 4

Picture credits
All photographs are from the Earthscape and ShutterStock picture libraries or from public domain sources.

This product is manufactured from sustainable managed forests. For every tree cut down at least one more is planted.

⚠ Understanding others

Remember that other people's beliefs are important to them. You must always be considerate and understanding when studying about faith.

Contents

As you go through the book, look for words in **BOLD CAPITALS**. These words are defined in the glossary.

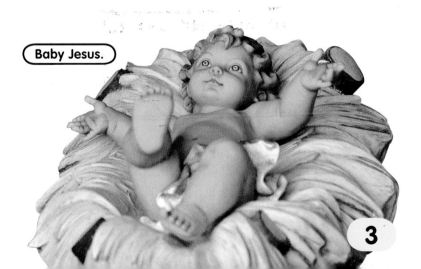

Baby Jesus.

3

Jesus is baptised by John.

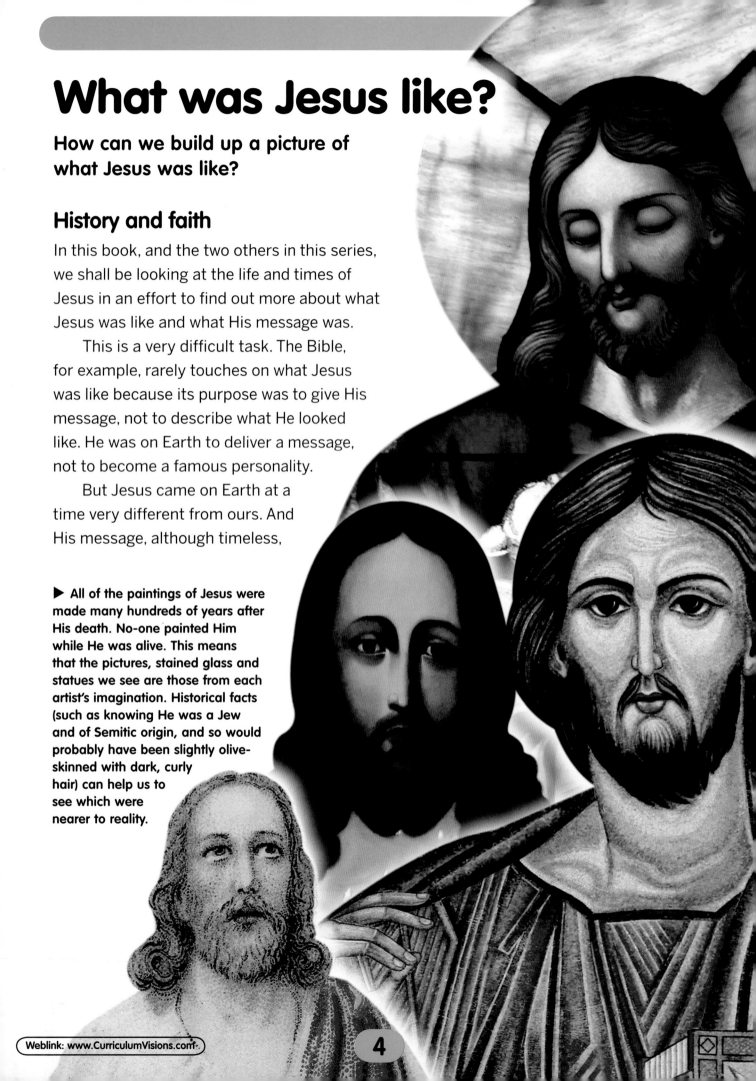

What was Jesus like?

How can we build up a picture of what Jesus was like?

History and faith

In this book, and the two others in this series, we shall be looking at the life and times of Jesus in an effort to find out more about what Jesus was like and what His message was.

This is a very difficult task. The Bible, for example, rarely touches on what Jesus was like because its purpose was to give His message, not to describe what He looked like. He was on Earth to deliver a message, not to become a famous personality.

But Jesus came on Earth at a time very different from ours. And His message, although timeless,

▶ All of the paintings of Jesus were made many hundreds of years after His death. No-one painted Him while He was alive. This means that the pictures, stained glass and statues we see are those from each artist's imagination. Historical facts (such as knowing He was a Jew and of Semitic origin, and so would probably have been slightly olive-skinned with dark, curly hair) can help us to see which were nearer to reality.

was set in the time He gave it. So, in order to understand Jesus better, we need to know what He said and did, but also what the Holy Land was like at the time.

The other thing you must understand is that this unique story has two quite different parts. One part is the simple historical fact that Jesus was born, lived and was eventually executed in the Holy Land. There can be no argument over that. The other part is that the accounts we have of Jesus tell us that He was involved in many things for which there is no historical evidence. Many of these are called miracles. Jesus also talked of God. These are matters of faith, rather than history. These books write about them as though they were true, but you must make up your own mind.

So now you know where our story was set and to whom most of what Jesus said was meant. Now we can start to tell the story, beginning at the beginning with the birth of Jesus. To do that we have first to understand what it was like to be born into this troubled corner of the Roman Empire...

5

Where Jesus was born

The land where Jesus grew up was not an easy place to live.

The land around Jerusalem is a hilly, almost mountainous land in the **MIDDLE EAST**. In the time of Jesus it was called Judea. Now it is partly in Israel and partly in Palestine. It has long, dry and very hot summers, making it seem almost like a desert. Nevertheless, winters are wet and cold and it is not uncommon for snow to fall.

A land of olives and goats

At the time of Jesus, most people were farmers. Remember this is hilly land in a region that gets no summer rain. So, many crops that need summer water will not grow. In the area that we are talking about – called Judea – the main farm products were olives, figs, dates and grapes (for wine), and the main domestic animals were goats, because they could survive best in this near-desert land. This modern picture still gives a good idea of what it must have been like in the time of Jesus. The tree is an olive tree. The animals are goats.

7

Jerusalem

Jerusalem is a city built on several hills.

Jerusalem was the largest city in Roman Palestine and home to about 80,000 people. It was what we would nowadays call a **COSMOPOLITAN** city, meaning a place where peoples from many parts of the world lived together.

Jerusalem was important enough to be where Roman soldiers were based. They lived in a fort in the centre of the city.

Jesus came into the world at a time when the Middle East was an unsettled place, just as it is today. In the days of Jesus, it was a time of turmoil because the land where most Jewish people lived was part of the Roman Empire, and the Jews didn't like it. So there was always tension in the air, and sometimes there were riots and rebellions.

Jews and Roman soldiers were not the only people in the city. A large number of Greeks lived there as well, because Palestine had been conquered by the Greeks three hundred years earlier under Alexander the Great. So, even at the time of Jesus' birth, hundreds of years later, many people followed Greek customs and even used Greek as their first language.

▼ A general view of modern Jerusalem. Solomon's Temple was built on the Temple Mount (hill). It is where the Golden Dome is now. The city walls enclosed the Old City as they still do today. Outside the city was the Mount of Olives, whose sides are still covered in olive groves. Another important hill for our story was also outside the Old City walls of the time. It is known as Golgotha, or Calvary, and it was the place where people were executed.

▼ The remains of an Old City gate.

Inside Jerusalem

Jerusalem was a maze of tiny alleyways.

Jerusalem was crowded inside its walls. In the time of Jesus the walls covered a smaller area than they do today. The way people got around in this cramped space was through a maze of tiny alleyways.

In some parts of the city the wealthy people lived in homes of stone. In other areas poor people lived in houses made of mud. In the heat of the summer it must have been a very exhausting place to live, and this kind of atmosphere makes people irritable and quarrelsome.

The only open space in the city was the area of the Temple Mount hill, which was occupied by the Jewish Temple and the Roman fort.

Priests and rabbis

Jerusalem, with its tightly-packed homes was a place of gossip. Anything that was happening soon got around. It was also a place of religious rivals.

At the time of Jesus, there were two groups of religious leaders fighting for people's hearts and minds. The traditionalists were the priests – the Sadducees. Every Jewish family had to pay the priests to make **SACRIFICES** at the Temple in Jerusalem on their behalf. It was good business and many Sadducee families were rich.

The Temple priests found themselves opposed by a party made up of teachers (**RABBIS**) who knew much about the Jewish law but who were not priests.

The Sadducees dismissed their opponents as Pharisees – a word meaning 'people who stray from the true path'. The teachers proudly adopted this abusive name and became leaders of the synagogue as opposed to the Temple controlled by the Sadducees. Jews had three main holy days (Passover, Shavuot and Sukkot) when everyone had to make a pilgrimage to the Temple. Jewish law required that animal and grain offerings should be 'unblemished' when brought into the Temple.

Rather than risk spoilage along the way, most pilgrims bought fresh items in the holy city. This was very good business for farmers for miles around.

Local merchants bought produce from the farmers and had licences to sell sacrificial animals and grain at a high price. So they made money from the pilgrims who came to the Temple, too.

Then the head of each family also had to pay a yearly temple tax. So, overall, the Temple was a huge money spinner for many people. The Sadduccees, merchants and farmers were determined to keep it this way. The Pharisees wanted change. As we shall see, the acts of Jesus matched the reform ideas of the Pharisees and so put Him squarely against the Sadducees.

◀▶ Jewish people still visit the remains of the Temple (often known as the Wailing Wall) to pray.

13

Herod and the Temple

Herod was the King of Israel at the time of Jesus' birth.

In the year of Jesus' birth, Jews of Judea lived in the Roman Empire. The Romans had conquered the land some 57 years earlier.

Each part of the Roman Empire was overseen by a Roman governor, but it was ruled on a day-to-day basis by local people. In 37 BC the Romans made Herod the King of Judea. The Romans thought of Judea as one of Rome's most rebellious possessions.

Herod was a Jew and he had to do a constant balancing act between his Jewish priests and Rome's demand that he control this troublesome region. In fact, from this point of view, Herod did his job well, leaving the Jews free to practise their religion, yet keeping peace in the region.

Herod was a great admirer of all things Roman and Greek and wanted to show that he could build monuments

as great as anyone. One of the important things he did in our story was to rebuild the Jewish Temple in Jerusalem.

The Temple was originally founded by King David (of the Old Testament) and finished by his son King Solomon. It is often called Solomon's Temple. This is where the Ark of the Covenant (the box with the Ten Commandments inside) was kept until it was lost many centuries later during a time when Jerusalem was attacked by the Babylonians.

As a result, the temple at Jerusalem – Solomon's Temple – was the holiest place for Jews even though, by Herod's time, it had lain in ruins for centuries.

Herod was determined to rebuild the Temple and make it bigger than ever. In fact, he built one of the most magnificent buildings of its time, covering twice the area of Solomon's Temple.

You need to remember this because the Temple in Jerusalem is where many of the important events in the first and last days of Jesus' life took place.

Herod didn't get to his position by being nice. In fact, he was a very ruthless and violent person. He could also be very jealous. He commanded the deaths of thousands of people during his battle for power. He was also afraid that people might take power away from him and, as a result, he would become especially afraid of the baby Jesus.

◀ This is a model of the Temple in Jerusalem as reconstructed by Herod. It is the 'stage' against which many of the great events of Jesus' life were played out. Notice it has an enormous courtyard, with the building called the Holy of Holies (representing the place where the Ark was once kept) in the centre. By the time of Jesus this building was also used (as Greeks and Romans used their temples) as a treasury, a kind of bank, where the wealth of Jewish people was kept. In Herod's day, the courtyard would have been full of people, many selling items to religious tourists (pilgrims).

Weblink: www.CurriculumVisions.com

What were Jesus' parents like?

The Bible tells us that Jesus is the son of God, but He also had parents on Earth: Mary and Joseph.

Joseph, who would be Jesus' earthly father, was descended from the royal line of Abraham and King David, important founders of the Jewish way of life. It was Abraham who made an agreement with God to worship only God, and it was he who established the Hebrew people. It was David who founded the Temple at Jerusalem. So, even though Joseph was only a carpenter, he was related to Abraham and David. This is very important because the Old Testament of the Bible says that the **SAVIOUR** would be related to David.

Mary

Strangely, the Bible does not tell us much about Mary. We first learn about Mary when Mary and Joseph's parents arranged their marriage – arranged marriages were common at the time. Mary was still a teenager – but it was also common for women to be married when still very young. This was because people did not expect to live much beyond their thirties, so it was important that a family was got under way quickly.

▶ Mary and Joseph as shown in this 19th century stained glass window. Notice that in this picture all the figures are shown as though they were northwest European, not Middle Eastern. This was very common until the 20th century.

The Annunciation

When Mary was engaged to Joseph, but before they were married, the **ANGEL** Gabriel came to her and told her that she would soon have a baby and that she should name the child Jesus. Mary was understandably petrified. Becoming pregnant out of marriage would have been a terrible thing for people of the time – the woman's father could even have had her killed or sold into slavery. So you can imagine how worried Joseph must have been when he discovered she was pregnant.

Then the angel appeared to Joseph, too, to explain what was about to happen. Although Joseph and Mary were very confused about what was going on, they trusted in God and the angel.

They had to find a way of doing God's will without upsetting the society in which they lived. Joseph decided to send Mary away in secret so she would not face the anger of the community.

▲ A Victorian postcard of the Annunciation angel.

Mary was greatly troubled at his words and wondered what kind of greeting this might be. But the angel said to her, "Do not be afraid, Mary, you have found favour with God. You will be with child and give birth to a son, and you are to give Him the name Jesus. He will be great and will be called the Son of the Most High. The Lord God will give Him the throne of His father David, and He will reign over the house of Jacob forever; His Kingdom will never end."

"How will this be," Mary asked the angel, "since I am a virgin?"

The angel answered, "The Holy Spirit will come upon you, and the power of the Most High will overshadow you. The holy one to be born will be called the Son of God. Even Elizabeth your relative is going to have a child in her old age, and she who was said to be barren is in her sixth month. For nothing is impossible with God."

"I am the Lord's servant," Mary answered. "May it be to me as you have said." Then the angel left her.

▲ This is what the Bible says about the conversation between Gabriel and Mary in the book of *Luke, Chapter 1*. It is a moment called the Annunciation.

▶ This is what the Bible says about the conversation between the angel and Joseph.

"Joseph, her husband, being a righteous man, and not willing to make her a public example, intended to put her away secretly."

Then, while Joseph was sleeping restlessly, worrying about what to do for Mary, an angel appeared to him in his dream. The angel told him that Mary's child was the Son of God who would save His people from their sins.

The birth of Jesus

Why Jesus of Nazareth was born in Bethlehem.

Just about the time when Mary was about to give birth to Jesus, the Romans decided to count all of the people in Israel so they knew how much tax to expect. As a result, everyone had to go back to the home town of the head of the household, so that each family could be counted.

Mary and Joseph had to travel from Nazareth, where they lived, to Joseph's home town of Bethlehem to be counted in the CENSUS.

Going to Bethlehem

Bethlehem is about 10 kilometres south of Jerusalem. Like Jerusalem it is up in the mountains, so it would have been cold and possibly snowy if December was the month when Jesus was born.

▼ This is how the Bible tells it. (Note that one of the provinces of Israel is called Galilee, which is where Nazareth was, and another region was called Judea, which is where Bethlehem was.)

Nazareth is nowhere near Bethlehem, however. To get to Bethlehem from Nazareth they had a 150 kilometre trip on foot. This would have been a terrible journey for someone who was just about to have a child. Like everyone else, they would have walked, although possibly Mary may have been seated on a donkey to make things a little easier.

Somewhere to stay

There would have been many people on the road, going to their home towns for the census. Joseph and Mary did not actually have any close family left in Bethlehem, but as it was Joseph's home town they may have stayed with distant relatives (this is what is often called 'staying at the inn').

With everyone on the road travelling, it was a very busy time and when Joseph and Mary got to Bethlehem there was no comfortable place for them to stay. In those days people lived with their animals. Some lived in mud or stone houses and others lived in caves in the rocky hillside.

Luke 2:1–7

Now it happened in those days, that a decree went out from Caesar Augustus that all the world should be enrolled. ... All went to enrol themselves, everyone to his own city. Joseph also went up from Galilee, out of the city of Nazareth, into Judea, to the city of David, which is called Bethlehem, because he was of the house and family of David; to enrol himself with Mary, who was pledged to be married to him as wife, being pregnant.

It happened, while they were there, that the day had come that she should give birth. She brought forth her first-born son, and she wrapped Him in bands of cloth, and laid Him in a feeding trough, because there was no room for them in the inn.

Inside the single-roomed home the family usually lived on a raised area and the animals lived below. With the normal raised living space full, Joseph and Mary probably had to make do with a space on the lower floor among the animals. This is probably why, when Mary gave birth, there were animals nearby.

The manger

You have to remember that people of that time were used to much harsher living conditions than we are today. Women often carried on working in the fields and simply walked to the side of the field to give birth.

▲ The hills of Judea can be very cold in winter. Here is a picture of Jerusalem with snow covering houses and fields. It might have been just like the time when Mary and Joseph went to nearby Bethlehem.

So no-one expected there to be any special arrangements for giving birth. Nevertheless, after Mary gave birth to Jesus, she still had to find a place to put Him down comfortably. Probably the only place He would not be trampled by the animals was in an animal feeding trough full of hay – known as a manger. She wrapped Him up in cloths (in **SWADDLING CLOTHES**) and placed Him in the manger, using the hay as a kind of soft bedding.

◀ It is hard for us to imagine the simple lives that people lived. This picture shows some of the cave homes around Bethlehem. Jesus may even have been born in one.

19

Weblink: www.CurriculumVisions.com

The Nativity

The Nativity is the account of the birth of Jesus of Nazareth.

▲ At the time of the birth, Mary and Joseph probably shared the bottom of a farmhouse with animals. Notice the yellow discs around the heads which are symbols used to tell us that these are holy people. This symbol is called a halo. Notice that in this picture the birth has taken place in a cave.

The previous pages have set out the background to the events of the birth of Jesus. But it was a momentous occasion and the Bible accounts tell us about it in much detail. This is what happened next.

The shepherds

Joseph and Mary seemed quite unremarkable. So there was absolutely no reason why anyone should want to visit them. Yet, just after Jesus was born, some shepherds came to the house they were staying in specifically to see the baby. Why should they have done that?

Of course, in the normal course of events, they would be out in the fields looking after their flocks (remember that at this time there were no fenced fields, so people always stayed with their animals).

There was no-one to come and tell them about Joseph and Mary. The Bible is quite clear: the shepherds had been visited by an angel while they were

▲ This is a model which tries to give a cave-like atmosphere to the Nativity scene. It shows the shepherds (left) who had come to visit and worship the baby, soon after the birth.

tending their flocks. The angel told them that if they went to Bethlehem they would find a baby, wrapped in swaddling clothes and lying in a feeding trough (manger), who was to become the Saviour of the world, Christ the Lord. So this is why the Bible tells us the shepherds hurried into the town and found the baby, and why they knew about Him and His future.

In a Nativity scene people try to recreate the birth of Jesus for Christmas celebrations.

Many Nativity scenes show Jesus in a wooden house (there was little spare wood in Judea) and sometimes in an inn. But, as we have seen, houses in Bethlehem at the time, were not like this. Jesus may even have been born in a house that partly used a natural cave as part of its living space.

The shepherds and the Three Wise Men are often shown in the same scene, but, as we shall see, they arrived at separate times. The shepherds were first. However, remember that in many models and paintings, the artist was helping people who could not read to understand the basic message and for this they needed to get the whole story into one convenient place, which is why some liberty was taken with the facts.

The Magi – the Three Wise Men

The shepherds were not the only visitors. A few days later, some travellers (often called the 'Three Wise Men', the '**Magi**', the 'Three Kings', or 'Kings from the east') came to visit Jesus in Bethlehem. This visit is now celebrated by the Christian festival called Epiphany.

To understand them we need to know that the word Magi means a priest from a sect that worshipped in what is modern Iran and India. As part of their religion, these particular priests learned to read the stars.

As it happened, modern astronomers can turn back the pages of history and find out what the stars were doing around the time of Jesus' birth.

You may need to know that Jesus was born about 6 BC in our calendar because people in the past made a mistake in their dates. If astronomers go back to 6 BC (see box: 'The birth of Jesus', opposite) they see something remarkable: the giant planet Jupiter close to the next largest planet, Saturn. This is a very rare event and may have looked like a star. Matthew tells us they navigated by following a bright star, which is the one Christians now call the Star of Bethlehem. It may also have been a comet.

◄ This is the place (marked by a metal star) that is traditionally thought of as the birthplace of Jesus. It is in the Church of the Nativity in Bethlehem.

The event could be seen some months before the birth, so they saw the sign and began to make plans. But they had a long way to go and they were venturing into a land unfamiliar to them.

These highly-regarded people would have been dressed in good clothes and would have looked different from the local people in Palestine. Anyone who met them would soon have regarded them as wise, and their dress would have suggested wealth, or kings.

The Bible never tells us how many people came from the east. It simply says there were three gifts brought and so people assume that a separate gift was brought by each person. If this is right then three people visited.

The Gospel of Matthew tells us that they came "from the east to Jerusalem" to worship the Christ, "born King of the Jews". So, having worked out that this event was to take place, they then had to find exactly where it was to be.

◄ This is a modern reconstruction of the Nativity with the Magi. Jesus is shown as a fair-haired baby, something that would not have been likely as He was a Middle-Eastern Jew. This reconstruction has used the idea that one of the Magi is black, but otherwise the Magi are Western European, whereas it is most likely they came from Iran or India. The picture tried to show the star in the east, but this has meant putting the whole scene out in the open. It is artistic licence to make the point of the story and not to be interpreted strictly.

The birth of Jesus

The GOSPELS do not mention a date or time for the birth of Jesus. The Western date of 25 December has been used only since about the 3rd century. Before then, Jesus' birth was generally celebrated on 6 January as part of the feast of Epiphany. This is still the date used by the Eastern church.

The Gospel of Matthew tells us that Jesus' birth occurred under the reign of Herod the Great, who died in 4 BC and scholars therefore believe that Jesus was born between 6-4 BC, most likely 6 BC.

The Nativity in art and music

Many people have tried to portray the baby Jesus in both art and music.

There are many ways in which we can imagine Jesus as a baby and the environment in which He was born. But the **GOSPELS** give us little to go on. As a result, down the ages, although the paintings and sculptures of the Nativity are based on the descriptions in the Bible,

◄ The Adoration of the Magi 1619, Hendrick ter Brugghen. Notice that the people are dressed in costumes of the 17th century, not costumes appropriate to the date of the birth of Jesus.

▲ Over the centuries, more figures were added to the Nativity scene.

in the Gospels of Matthew and Luke, these written accounts have then been developed, according to what people thought in the centuries that followed.

You can find the Nativity as murals (wall paintings), panel paintings, pictures inside ancient books (manuscript illuminations), stained glass windows and paintings on canvas. The most common place to find these paintings is behind the altar, often as a mixture of painting and sculpture.

Part of the purpose of a painting is to tell a story with symbols that are well understood. For example, for two thousand years before the Birth of Christ, the pharaohs of Egypt had been shown seated while people brought gifts to them.

It was the same in Roman times, when defeated peoples brought gifts to a seated emperor. So a seated person showed power and authority. It is for this reason that early painters showed the Magi holding their gifts in front of them, facing a seated Virgin with Christ on her lap. It was a tradition of the Middle East and everyone understood what it meant.

The earliest pictures of the Nativity show the infant, tightly wrapped, with an ox and an ass nearby. These are not mentioned in the Gospel but in the Old Testament, for example, *Isaiah 1.3*: "The ox knoweth his owner, and the ass his master's crib" So people painted in what they felt explained an ancient **PROPHECY**.

25

Weblink: www.CurriculumVisions.com

By the 6th century the setting was changed to a cave, which as we have seen is entirely possible, and this is still how the Nativity is shown in Eastern Orthodox churches. Mary is shown recovering beside the infant, who is on a raised area, whilst Joseph rests his head on his hand in the foreground (bottom left in the picture above).

These and recreations (mystery plays) of the Nativity in the Middle Ages, also show midwives, including Salome. The Magi may be shown approaching at the top left on horseback, and the shepherds at the right of the cave. The scene is completed by angels.

The West used many of the same characters, but kept to the idea of the (Western) stable and there are no midwives except in Italian paintings.

Following the birth, Mary and Joseph kneel to pray to the child. This time is known as the Adoration of the Child and is often used in paintings.

◀▼ The Nativity in a cave (left) as shown by Eastern Orthodox belief, and in a wooden stable (below), often shown in Western churches.

What was baby Jesus like?

As you have read, we know very little about what Jesus was like as a baby. But we do know that He was born of Jewish parents in Israel, so He would have looked like other Jewish people of the region, that is He would have had dark, perhaps curly, hair and He would have had a slightly olive or brown skin colour. If you think about the purpose of Jesus coming into the world, there is absolutely no reason to suppose that He was beautiful. In fact being rather ordinary would have been more suitable as people could then have related to Him for what He had to say, rather than following Him because He was some kind of supermodel. But remember, that in our age we are keen to know as much of the truth and real world as we can. In the past this is not what people wanted to do, which, as we have shown, is why ancient pictures are often very different from those made in modern times.

Music

Very often a scene can be represented and given feeling in music, a kind of musical picture. Nowhere is this more so than in the Nativity. Many people have been inspired by music and, of course, by visiting the holy site.

Phillips Brooks was an Episcopal priest who was inspired by his visit to Bethlehem in 1865. He wrote the *O little town of Bethlehem* poem for his church.

Silent night is another popular Christmas carol commemorating the birth of Jesus and the Nativity. It was written as *Stille nacht* in German by the Austrian priest Father Josef Mohr and first performed in 1818 to be accompanied by a guitar.

Silent night, holy night.
All is calm, all is bright
Round yon virgin mother and child
Holy infant so tender and mild
Sleep in heavenly peace
Sleep in heavenly peace

Silent night, holy night.
Shepherds quake at the sight,
Glories stream from Heaven afar,
Heav'nly hosts sing alleluia:
Christ the Saviour is born,
Christ the Saviour is born.

Silent night, holy night
Son of God, love's pure light,
Radiant beams from Thy holy face,
With the dawn of redeeming grace:
Jesus, Lord, at Thy birth,
Jesus, Lord, at Thy birth.

O little town of Bethlehem,
How still we see thee lie!
Above thy deep and dreamless sleep
The silent stars go by;

Yet in thy dark streets shineth
The everlasting Light;
The hopes and fears of all the years
Are met in thee tonight.

O morning stars, together
Proclaim the holy birth!
And praises sing to God the King,
And peace to men on Earth.

For Christ is born of Mary,
And gathered all above,
While mortals sleep, the angels keep
Their watch of wondering love.

How silently, how silently,
The wondrous gift is given!
So God imparts to human hearts
The blessings of His Heaven.

No ear may hear His coming,
But in this world of sin,
Where meek souls will receive Him, still
The dear Christ enters in.

Where children pure and happy
Pray to the blessed Child,
Where misery cries out to Thee,
Son of the mother mild;

Where charity stands watching
And faith holds wide the door,
The dark night wakes, the glory breaks,
And Christmas comes once more.

O holy Child of Bethlehem!
Descend to us, we pray;
Cast out our sin and enter in,
Be born in us today.

We hear the Christmas angels
The great glad tidings tell;
O come to us, abide with us,
Our Lord Emmanuel!

The Massacre of the Innocents

The Three Wise men had to visit King Herod to get directions. But Herod knew nothing about the holy birth. The possibility of a king made him anxious.

The Wise Men knew of their quest, but they would not have been able to pinpoint the exact place from just a star. So, being high caste people, they did the obvious thing and went to ask King Herod, as they assumed he, too, would welcome the news. How wrong they turned out to be.

When Herod heard the news he appeared in public to agree with the Magi that this was wonderful news. But actually he was very upset, because he did not want any trouble in his kingdom or anyone challenging his rule. He gathered all the chief priests and scribes and asked them where the Saviour would be born. They told him in Bethlehem, because it was written in the Jewish holy books:

"Out of you, Bethlehem, shall come forth a governor, who shall shepherd My people, Israel."

Herod was cunning. He told the Wise Men what the scriptures had said and so to go to Bethlehem. Herod then asked that he might be told if they found the Christ Child. The Magi eventually reached the place where Jesus was and saw the young child with Mary, and they fell down and worshipped Him. Opening their treasures, they offered to Him symbolic gifts: gold, frankincense and myrrh.

Then the Magi were warned in dreams about Herod's deadly intentions for the child and they decided to return home by a different route, in order to stop him killing Jesus. So that left Herod with a problem. He knew there was a child, but he could not pinpoint which one it was.

▼ The Massacre of the Innocents is shown in this sculpture. Mary and Joseph (shown with halos) are taking Jesus off to Egypt. Almost out of sight on the left of this picture, Herod has commanded all first born to be slaughtered (inset).

At the Temple

While Herod was pondering what to do, Joseph, with Mary, took Jesus to the Temple in nearby Jerusalem, as required by Jewish law, so He could be properly admitted to the Jewish religion. But things were about to get a bit complicated. When Mary and Joseph arrived at the Temple, there was a man there called Simeon. The Holy Spirit had told Simeon that he would see the Christ before he died. When Simeon saw baby Jesus in the Temple, he knew that this was the Saviour. He picked the baby Jesus up and blessed God and said (*Luke 2:21–40*) "Now You are releasing Your servant, Master, according to Your word, in peace; for my eyes have seen Your salvation, which

You have prepared before the face of all peoples; a light for revelation to the nations, and the glory of Your people Israel."

Just then a prophetess called Anna, who was very old, came up to Joseph and Mary. Anna never left the Temple, and spent all her time in worship and prayer. When Anna saw Jesus, she also gave thanks to the Lord and said that Jesus would bring redemption to the Jewish people. So here were yet more people who recognised the **MESSIAH** without having been told. Of course, this kind of story was important news and spread quickly.

The Massacre of the Innocents

By now Herod had become suspicious that the Magi had not returned to tell him where Jesus was, and there were stories of the Messiah abroad. Unable to find out exactly where Jesus was, Herod ordered that all the first-born male young children in Bethlehem be killed. This is known as the Massacre of the Innocents.

So how was it that Jesus was not killed at this time? Of course, it costs money to stay away from home and Joseph was earning nothing while he was away from his work. So the family soon left Bethlehem and were not there when Herod ordered the massacre.

Mary and Joseph did not know that their son was still at risk, but an angel told them to go to Egypt instead of going home and they obeyed. This kept them safely away from Herod until, later that year, he died. Joseph got work there and they then returned to Nazareth, fulfilling the prophecy of the Old Testament: "Out of Egypt I called My Son."

Weblink: www.CurriculumVisions.com

What was young Jesus like?

Jesus had a normal country upbringing, but it was already clear to those around that here was someone who was very special.

Of all the stages of the life of Jesus, we know least about what happened to Him as He grew up. The Gospels are interested in the great things that Jesus did as a teacher, rather than telling us about His life as a boy. But, as you will know, you learn a lot as you grow up. You find out how to live with people, how to respect them, and above all, you learn that there are many types of people with many fears.

◀ Artists have usually not made pictures of Jesus as a young boy. They are almost always of Jesus as a baby with His mother. Such works are generally referred to as the "MADONNA and Child" or "Virgin and Child". They do not represent any particular event, but are used to help people focus their prayers.

A carpenter's son

In the time of Jesus, nothing much changed. That is, everything was based upon tradition. Roles and rituals were passed down from many generations beforehand. In Jesus' time, Nazareth was a small farming village of about 35 houses containing between 200 and 400 people whose days were all very similar. They were mainly worried about the things that still worry us: how to get enough food and how to keep their families safe.

Usually people wore a kind of long shirt made of wool. In winter, when it was cold, they also wore a loose fitting coat. You can still see exactly the same thing worn by Middle-Eastern farmers today. Shoes were usually sandals made of simple pieces of animal hide drawn together with laces. When they went inside, they took their sandals off. Travellers often carried their shoes instead of wearing them until they entered cities, so they could look their best in the city.

Men wore a square of cloth on their heads as protection against the strong sunshine and as part of their religious duty. Women also covered their heads.

Women prepared all of the food. Typically a family ate two meals: breakfast – light or small amounts of food, such as bread, figs, dates and fresh cheese, taken to work; and dinner – a larger meal which was mostly vegetables, fruits and eggs. Fish was common, as were stews and soups that would have been thickened with grain. Typical seasonings included salt, cumin, coriander, mint, dill and mustard. Food was sweetened with wild honey or syrups made from dates or grapes.

Houses were made from mud bricks and consisted of one or two rooms, and usually had earthen floors, flat roofs and wooden front doors. In summer people would sleep on the flat roofs during hot nights. Cooking was done outside, or in a separate building (there were no chimneys for the smoke to go out of). Water was carried in from a public well and stored in a courtyard cistern. At night, people used earthenware oil lamps. They slept on mats.

Nazareth was small because it didn't have a good water supply. There was only a single spring (now a shrine called 'Mary's Well'). Most people relied (as they do today) on sheep and goats grazing and browsing the tough leaves.

Learning

Any education children got was either at home, from their parents, or in the local synagogue from a rabbi. They may also have seen the wandering teachers and their students who followed a Greek tradition. This is what Jesus was to become.

It is likely that, as Jesus grew up and began to talk with others, He may have been regarded as some kind of genius because His knowledge grew much faster than the other people of His age.

▶ Jesus would have lived among other boys, helping His father at carpentry and probably also helping out with herding of sheep, just as is done near Nazareth today.

Jesus travels to Jerusalem

When Jesus was twelve He began to show signs of being the Saviour.

Jerusalem was the centre of the Jewish world. During the main religious festivals between 100,000 and 250,000 pilgrims would also stream down the long main road of the city.

The city was dominated by Herod's new Temple, with its sheer 50 m high walls that supported a great open space on the top of the hill called the Temple Mount. ("Look, Teacher, what large stones and what large buildings!" Gospel of Mark.)

At the time of Jesus there were seven entrances to the Temple Mount. Before buying an animal for sacrifice, visitors changed their Roman denarii (the pounds of the day) for shekels, or Temple coins, that had no portraits on them and so did not violate the Jewish prohibition on images of people.

Scholars stood on the steps to teach, surrounded by students, and preachers shouted out their sermons, in the hopes of gaining followers.

The Temple compound itself was more like a small city. There were thousands of priests, attendants, temple soldiers and servants.

▼ This stained glass window shows the young Jesus preaching in the Temple.

Jesus in the Temple

When Jesus was twelve, by the Jewish tradition, He became a man. In that year, Jesus' family went to the Temple to celebrate Passover and stayed for the seven days of the holiday.

The family left Jerusalem at the end of the holiday, travelling in a large group of relatives and acquaintances. Because they were in a large group, Joseph and Mary did not realise that Jesus had stayed behind in Jerusalem until they had been travelling for almost a whole day (they assumed He was with some other relative in the group).

When they realised Jesus was missing, Mary and Joseph returned to Jerusalem and searched for Him. After three days they found Him in the Temple, sitting in the middle of a group of religious teachers, and answering questions. Remember, He was still only twelve years old. All the teachers and people around Him were amazed that He knew so much religious law.

When Joseph and Mary saw Jesus, Mary said, "Son, why have You treated us this way? Your father and I were anxiously looking for You." At this, Jesus said, "Why were you looking for Me? Didn't you know that I must be in My Father's house?"

Mary and Joseph didn't really understand what Jesus was saying and they kept His remarks to themselves. Then they all went off to Nazareth where Jesus continued to work for His father and to be a normal member of society, although, of course, people continued to be amazed by His understanding of Jewish law when He was in the synagogue.

John the Baptist

The ministry of Jesus begins with His baptism by John.

The most important part of the life of Jesus is concerned with His teachings. This is called His ministry. Jesus did not teach until after His baptism, so baptism was one of the most important events in His story. So it is helpful if we first find out about John the Baptist, the person who baptised Jesus.

Troubled times

Jesus grew up during unsettled times for Judea. There was often violence as people rebelled against Roman rule and the Romans fought back. With so much turmoil and upheaval, many people were looking for a Saviour and believed in the prophecies that said a Saviour, or Messiah, would be coming soon. As a result of all this, there were many preachers around.

John was born about six months before Jesus. On the surface, John the Baptist seemed to be just another preacher. However, he had been sent by God to prepare people for the coming of Jesus.

John preached in the land around Judea. He lived a simple life. He wore simple clothing made up of a tunic of rough camel hair. He only ate foods that could be gathered from the desert, such as locusts and wild honey. He told people to ask God's forgiveness for their sins. He also baptised people in the River Jordan – saying prayers over them while immersing them in water. The water symbolised the washing away of past sins and a rebirth. It was not, of course, a symbol of Christianity at that time, but what Jews did to people when they converted to the Jewish faith.

John was not an easy man to have around. He followed the example of early Hebrew prophets, challenging sinful rulers, calling for repentance, and promising God's justice. Because of this, some people began to think that John might be a prophet, whose role was to announce the coming of the Messiah (Jesus). When people asked him, "Who are you?", he replied, "I am not the Christ." So they asked him, "What then? Are you Elijah? Why then do you baptise, if you are not the Christ, nor Elijah, nor the Prophet?"

John's reply was, "I baptise in water, but among you stands one whom you don't know. He is the one who comes after me, who is preferred before me, whose sandal strap I'm not worthy to loosen.

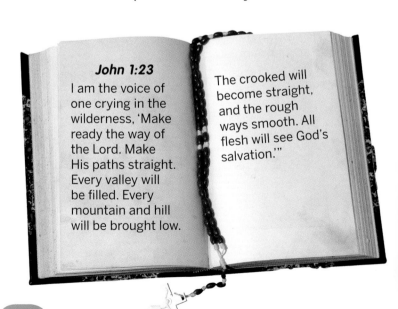

John 1:23
I am the voice of one crying in the wilderness, 'Make ready the way of the Lord. Make His paths straight. Every valley will be filled. Every mountain and hill will be brought low. The crooked will become straight, and the rough ways smooth. All flesh will see God's salvation.'"

The nature of baptism

Some Christians believe that Jesus is a natural-born man and His baptism is the point at which He came to embody the Holy Spirit. Many other Christians think of Jesus' baptism as being part of His human nature, rather than His divine nature.

In Eastern Christianity, Jesus' baptism is celebrated on 6 January, the feast of Epiphany. In the Roman Catholic Church and the Anglican Communion, it is celebrated in the following week, at the feast of the Baptism of the Lord.

In Roman Catholicism, the baptism of Jesus is the First Luminous Mystery (see box on page 37).

▲ The birthplace of John the Baptist. Notice the rocky walls of the cave still preserved in the upper picture.

▶ This is part of a map called the Madaba Map (and now preserved in the Greek Orthodox Basilica of Saint George in Madaba) which was made as a mosaic in Jordan in about the 6th century. All of the words are in Greek, as was usual at the time. It shows where John baptised near where the River Jordan enters the Dead Sea, south of Galilee. (Originally, the map measured 21m by 7m and contained over two million pieces.)

◀ Believers being rebaptised in the River Jordan at a place which is thought to be close to where Jesus was baptised.

Weblink: www.CurriculumVisions.com

Jesus is baptised

Jesus' ministry starts immediately after His baptism.

John baptised and preached that people had to repent before the Judgement Day. This was popular, and many people began to follow him. One day Jesus stood in amongst the crowd, waiting His turn to be baptised. John was not to know Jesus was in the queue. However, as soon as he saw Jesus, John announced that He was the Messiah.

John 1:28–34

John's immediate reaction was to tell the people waiting to be baptised that here was the 'Lamb of God, who takes away the sin of the world! This is He of whom I said, 'After me comes a man who is preferred before me, for He was before me.' I didn't know Him, but for this reason I came baptising in water: that He would be revealed to Israel." John testified, saying,

"I have seen the Spirit descending like a dove out of Heaven, and it remained on Him. I didn't recognise Him, but He who sent me to baptise in water, He said to me, 'On whomever you will see the Spirit descending, and remaining on Him, the same is He who baptises in the Holy Spirit.' I have seen, and have testified that this is the Son of God."

When Jesus asked John to baptise Him, John replied that it was Jesus who should be baptising him. But after this protest, John baptised Jesus as he had been asked.

Since the purpose of baptism is to wash away sin, and Jesus is without sin, it may seem odd that Jesus wanted to be baptised. But John was also sent by God to prepare the way for the Messiah, and so another way to look at John's baptism of Jesus is a sign of the end of Jesus' everyday life and the start of His ministry. Many Christians regard baptism as an adult as a symbol of having their previous sins washed away and being 'born again' following the example of Jesus.

We don't know exactly how John baptised people or what he said when he did it, but we can imagine that he waded into the River Jordan with them, said a few words about repenting sins in the eyes of God, and then momentarily held the person's head under the water.

How it really happened we shall never know, but the idea of baptism is central to what Christians believe.

As soon as He had been baptised, the Holy Spirit came to Jesus and told Him that He was the Son of God, and that God was pleased with Him. The Holy Spirit then instructed Jesus to go into the wilderness.

◄ A picture showing the baptism of Jesus in the River Jordan. In general, the tradition of Jewish purification was to immerse the person completely under the water and this is probably what happened to Jesus. The tradition of the early Christians, however, was to stand in water and for water to be poured over the upper body, often from a shell.

The First Luminous Mystery
THE BAPTISM OF THE LORD

❶ John is baptising in the Jordan proclaiming a baptism of repentance.

❷ "I am the voice of one crying in the desert, make straight the way of the Lord."

❸ "One mightier than I is coming after me."

❹ "I have baptised you with water, He will baptise you with the Holy Spirit."

❺ Seeing Jesus, John exclaims: "Behold the Lamb of God."

❻ After Jesus' baptism a voice from Heaven: "This is My beloved Son in whom I am well pleased."

❼ The Spirit descends upon Jesus in the form of a dove.

❽ In this heavenly manifestation is instituted the sacrament of baptism.

❾ The divine Trinity is manifested: the voice of the Father is heard as the Spirit descends upon the Son.

❿ Filled with the Holy Spirit, Jesus was led by the Spirit into the desert for 40 days.

From the wilderness to Galilee

Before Jesus began to preach around Galilee, He felt He needed to purify Himself by fasting, and prove His worth by rejecting the Devil.

After He was baptised, Jesus spent a long time in the wilderness away from all houses and farms. The New Testament uses the term 40 days, but that is a figure of speech and isn't meant to be taken literally.

Jesus wanted to cleanse His mind of all dark thoughts. But, of course, as we all know, dark thoughts come easily. When you are fasting, as Jesus decided to do, the mind is especially likely to have dark thoughts. So this was a great test.

What we call 'dark thoughts' nowadays, people used to call the 'thoughts of the Devil' or the 'thoughts of Satan'. The Gospels say that after Jesus had fasted for 40 days He was tempted by the Devil, who said. "If You are the Son of God, command this stone to become bread." But Jesus was not tempted. Instead He answered, "It is written, 'Man shall not live by bread alone, but by every word of God.'"

So the Devil tried again. He made Jesus imagine He was on a high mountain

and showed Him all the kingdoms of the world. The Devil then told Jesus that He could be the ruler of the world if He would worship the Devil. But Jesus was still not tempted and told the Devil, "Get thee behind Me Satan! For it is written, 'You shall worship the Lord your God, and Him only shall you serve.'"

Next, the Devil showed Jesus the Temple in Jerusalem and told Jesus that if He was indeed the Son of God, He should throw Himself from the top of the Temple and trust in the angels to save Him from being dashed on the stones below. But Jesus was still not tempted and told the Devil, "It has been said, 'You shall not tempt the Lord your God.'"

This was the last temptation. Jesus had resisted all of them, so the Devil left Him.

At long last, Jesus felt able to leave the wilderness and He began to preach.

Jesus' fasting became the model for the practice of fasting in Lent in the Roman Catholic and Eastern Orthodox churches.

Jesus makes His home in Galilee

After this, Jesus made His home in Capernaum (Kap-ur-nay-um), a fishing village of about 1,500 people, on the shores of the Sea of Galilee. It was quite an important place in its time and was even home to a Roman centurion.

This is where Jesus gathered His Disciples. He gathered them from the countryside. His power base were ordinary working people – quite unlike the wealthy Sadducees of Jerusalem.

39

Jesus begins to preach

After being baptised, Jesus started to preach in synagogues in the region called Galilee. This is how He began to build a following.

Jesus was a Jew, so, having grown to a man, He began to preach in the synagogues. On each Jewish Sabbath, a different part of the Jewish Bible is read out loud in the synagogue. Jesus mostly taught in the synagogue of Capernaum, where He lived. However, one Sabbath, Jesus went into the synagogue in Nazareth and stood up to read that week's part of the Jewish Bible,

which happened to be from the *Book of Isaiah* where it was written:

"The Spirit of the Lord is on me, because he has anointed me to preach good news to the poor. He has sent me to heal the brokenhearted, to proclaim release to the captives, recovering of sight to the blind, to deliver those who are crushed, and to proclaim the acceptable year of the Lord."

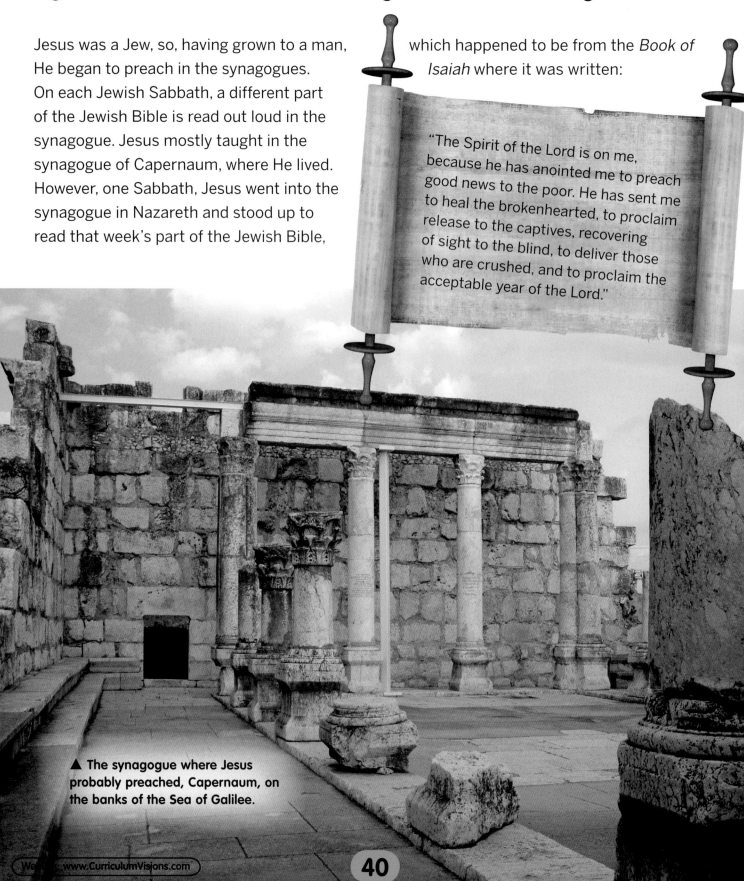

▲ The synagogue where Jesus probably preached, Capernaum, on the banks of the Sea of Galilee.

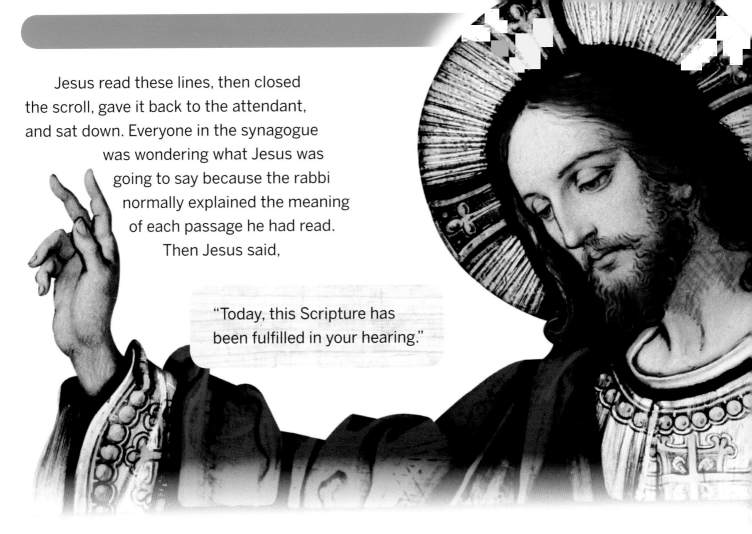

Jesus read these lines, then closed the scroll, gave it back to the attendant, and sat down. Everyone in the synagogue was wondering what Jesus was going to say because the rabbi normally explained the meaning of each passage he had read. Then Jesus said,

"Today, this Scripture has been fulfilled in your hearing."

At first the townspeople were impressed that Jesus had read so beautifully. Then they began to think about what Jesus had said. Gradually it dawned on them that the words He had just said meant that He was calling Himself the Messiah.

They knew Jesus as Joseph's son, and wondered how the son of an ordinary person from their town could dare to call Himself the Messiah. In reply, Jesus said that no prophet is accepted in his hometown, meaning that whenever a prophet comes along, the people who know him never believe that he is a prophet. And, of course, Jewish people still do not believe that Jesus was the Messiah.

Jesus then told them that in the Jewish Bible the prophets only help those who believe, and so the people of Nazareth will suffer if they do not listen to Him and repent of their sins.

Jesus also reminded them that, in the days of the prophets, when Elijah was healing people, he healed only one person with the disease called leprosy, and that person wasn't even a Jew, but a Syrian man. With this, Jesus seemed to be saying that He had been sent by God to preach not just to the leaders and the Jews, but to everyone.

When the people of Nazareth heard all this, many of them got very angry. They thought He was being **BLASPHEMOUS**, so they threw Jesus out of the synagogue.

A crowd of angry people tried to push Jesus to the top of the hill that Nazareth was built on – they wanted to throw Him off the cliff. But Jesus calmly walked through the crowd and went on His way. It was not to be the last time that a crowd got angry.

Weblink: www.CurriculumVisions.com

Gathering His followers

The Disciples were learners. The Apostles were messengers and they were the most important of Jesus' followers because He had a mission for them to do after He had died.

Disciples are people who learn. The word, which comes from the Greek, meaning 'learner', is used for the people who learned from Jesus during His ministry. Usually the 'Disciples' (with a capital D) are meant to be the same people who (with the exception of Judas) went on to be the Apostles. The Apostles first had to learn (that is they were disciples) before they could spread the teachings of Jesus (become apostles).

Jesus knew who He wanted as apostles and so He called them individually to be His Disciples.

The Gospels do mention how some of these Apostles came to be called by Jesus, and we'll discuss this next.

Jesus calls Simon and Andrew

One day, soon after He had returned from the desert and had begun preaching, Jesus was passing along the beach by the sea of Galilee at Bethsaida and He saw two fishermen, Simon (who Jesus renamed Peter, meaning 'rock') and his brother Andrew (which is a Greek name meaning valour), who were casting their fishing nets into the sea. When Jesus saw Simon and

◀ This stained glass window shows Jesus calling the first pair of Disciples, Simon and Andrew from their boat.

Andrew He said to them, "Come after Me, and I will make you into fishers of men."

They immediately left their nets and followed Him. This was a very important decision, especially since fishing was profitable, and required large start-up costs, so abandoning everything would have been an important sacrifice. Simon and Andrew abandoned their most important worldly possessions to follow Jesus. Later Christians have sometimes followed this model. For example, nuns and monks have very few personal possessions.

However, in the Gospel of Luke, Luke gives another reason why Simon Peter and Andrew were convinced so quickly to give up fishing. He writes that Jesus told Simon and his brother to put their nets in the water. Even though they caught nothing all day, they put their nets in the water and pulled them up full of fish. At this proof that Jesus was the Messiah, Simon and his brother immediately became followers of Jesus.

Jesus calls James and John

Very shortly after meeting Andrew and Simon, Jesus went to two more fishermen, twin brothers James and John. They were friends of Simon and Andrew and often worked as a team with them when fishing.

James and John were in their boat with their father, Zebedee, mending their fishing nets. When Jesus called to them to follow Him, they put down their nets and followed Jesus.

By leaving immediately, James and John were abandoning their father. This is very serious, and shows how devoted they were to Jesus and that they must have put their faith in God to see that their father was not left without help.

These first four Disciples were all fishermen from Bethsaida and it may be that Jesus knew them from before. Jesus worked as a carpenter, and we could imagine Him repairing fishing boats and meeting fishermen that way. That may be one reason why these four men were the first ones called by Jesus – because He knew them.

Philip and Bartholomew

Jesus was again walking by the sea where Philip was preparing to fish. Philip was another native of the fishing village of Bethsaida. Jesus simply said, "Follow Me." When he heard this, Philip went to his friend Bartholomew and told him that they had at last found the One of whom Moses and the Prophets wrote. "He is Jesus of Nazareth, the son of Joseph."

Because he knew Nazareth was a very small town, not known for much of anything, Bartholomew replied, "Can any good thing come out of Nazareth?"

Philip said to him, "Come and see."

When Jesus saw Bartholomew coming, He said, "Behold, an Israelite indeed, in whom is no deceit!" This was very high praise. Jesus meant that Bartholomew was a very good man and knew Jewish scripture very well.

Bartholomew then asked Jesus, "How do you know me?"

Jesus answered, "Before Philip called you, when you were under the fig tree, I saw you."

The phrase 'under the fig tree' is based on a Jewish figure of speech referring to studying the Jewish Bible or Torah. So it may be that Jesus knew of Bartholomew from the synagogue and

knew that he was a good scholar and very knowledgeable about religious matters.

Bartholomew was very impressed by Jesus and the way that Jesus knew who he was. He said, "Rabbi, You are the Son of God! You are King of Israel!"

Jesus answered him, "Because I told you, 'I saw you underneath the fig tree,' do you believe? You will see greater things than these!" Jesus meant that knowing Bartholomew was a good scholar was nothing special and that Jesus would show Bartholomew many miracles. "You will see Heaven opened, and the angels of God ascending and descending on the Son of Man."

▲ The Sea of Galilee.

So Philip and Bartholomew also became Jesus' Disciples.

Matthew

Jesus then called Matthew as His Disciple. He is the last Disciple for whom we have an independent story telling how he became an Apostle. We know little about some of the others.

Jesus was walking by the seaside, surrounded by people who He was preaching to. However, all of a sudden He called to the tax collector Matthew and simply said "Follow Me." Matthew immediately got up and followed Jesus.

Most Jews considered tax collectors to be traitors because they collected money on behalf of the Romans, so they were often shunned (avoided). So, by asking Matthew to follow Him, Jesus was showing people that everyone is equally welcome in the Kingdom of God.

Shortly after this, Matthew invited Jesus and many of His followers to his house for dinner. There were other tax collectors there, and other people, followers of Jesus, who were thought of as 'sinners'. When the local religious leaders learned of this, they came to the house and asked Jesus what He was doing, eating dinner with sinners and tax collectors. Jesus said to them, "Those who are healthy have no need for a doctor, but those who are sick do. I have not come to call the righteous, but sinners to repentance."

This angered the religious authorities, who felt it was blasphemous.

Jesus gathers the final Disciples

Quite soon after, Jesus had gathered all twelve of the people He wanted to be Disciples. The twelve were:

1. Simon, renamed Peter
2. Andrew, the brother of Simon Peter
3. James, son of Zebedee
4. John (the brother of James)
5. Philip
6. Bartholomew (also called Nathanael)
7. Matthew the tax collector (also called Levi)
8. Thomas
9. James, son of Alphaeus
10. Simon
11. Jude (Thaddaeus)
12. Judas Iscariot, who later betrayed Jesus

Jesus later appointed these twelve as His Apostles. Their task was to start the Christian church. However, as you will discover, Judas betrayed Jesus and then killed himself, so, after Jesus' death, the Apostles chose Matthias to replace him.

Jesus asked the Disciples to join Him on a mountain. This is a symbol, because in the Old Testament (the Jewish Bible), mountains were places where God sometimes spoke to prophets, such as Moses talking to God on Mount Sinai. At Sinai there were twelve tribes of the Hebrews; here there are twelve Disciples. At Sinai, Moses received the laws directly from God; here, the Disciples receive power and authority from Jesus, the Son of God.

Capernaum and Bethsaida

Bethsaida was the beach area of Capernaum. It was surrounded by poor grazing land and mostly occupied by fishermen who kept their boats on the beach. It was a place renowned for good fish catches. Here Philip, Andrew, Simon Peter and perhaps also James and John were born and lived. The house of Andrew and Simon Peter was near the synagogue in Capernaum.

▲ Ruins of the first church built at Capernaum over the home of Simon Peter (St Peter). The ruins are kept under a glass roof inside a modern church (upper picture).

When He had gathered them together, Jesus authorised His Apostles to do three things: preach, heal sickness, and cast out devils. These are three things which Jesus had been doing Himself, so He was entrusting them with continuing His mission (knowing, therefore, that it was soon to end). There is, however, one notable absence: forgiving sins. This is something which Jesus had done, but not something the Apostles were allowed to do until after Jesus' Resurrection.

The next stage

In this book we have seen how Jesus was born, how He escaped being murdered when He was a baby, how He grew up in a normal household and then, being so obviously knowledgeable about religion, became a rabbi, a teacher. We saw how He was baptised and then how He began to gather His Disciples. In the next book we look at the important next stage of His life: His teachings and actions, including the miracles.

Weblink: www.CurriculumVisions.com

Glossary

ANGEL A spiritual messenger from God.

BLASPHEMOUS The disrespectful use of the name of God.

CENSUS An official population count.

COSMOPOLITAN Made up of people from many parts of the world.

GOSPEL The 'Good News'. The first four books of the New Testament: the Gospel of Matthew, Gospel of Mark, Gospel of Luke and Gospel of John.

MADONNA A word for the mother of Jesus.

MAGI Ancient knowledgeable people who studied the stars.

MESSIAH Jewish word for the saviour of Israel. The Greek word is Christ.

MIDDLE EAST The area from the eastern end of the Mediterranean sea to the border of Pakistan, and including northeastern Africa.

PROPHECY A revelation by God to a prophet, a person who then tells of some future important event.

RABBI A Jewish religious teacher. Also used to mean someone superior to yourself.

SACRIFICE To make something sacred by offering food, valuable objects or the lives of animals as an act of worship.

SAVIOUR A person who helps people achieve Salvation.

SWADDLING CLOTHES A traditional method of wrapping infants tightly in sheets of cloth or blankets.

Index